SPY UNIVERSITY

The Spy's Guide to Surveillance

BY **JimWiese** WITH **H.KeithMelton**
SPY EXPERT

SCHOLASTIC INC.

NEW YORK TORONTO LONDON AUCKLAND SYDNEY
MEXICO CITY NEW DELHI HONG KONG BUENOS AIRES

This Minox Model B camera, a favorite among spies around the world, was produced from 1958 to 1972. It was popular because it didn't require any batteries. Minox cameras continued to be used widely until the 1990s.

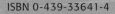

ISBN 0-439-33641-4

Copyright © 2002 by Scholastic Inc.

Editor: Andrea Menotti
Designers: Robert Rath, Lee Kaplan   Illustrations: Daniel Aycock
Photos: www.spyimages.net

12 11 10 9 8 7 6 5   2 3 4 5 6 7 / 0

Printed in the U.S.A.

First Scholastic printing, November 2002

The publisher has made every effort to ensure that the activities in this book are safe when done as instructed. Children are encouraged to do their spy activities with willing friends and family members and to respect others' right to privacy. Adults should provide guidance and supervision whenever the activity requires.

TABLE OF Contents

 This means you'll use this month's Spy Gear in this activity.

 This means you can find a related activity on the Spy University web site.

SEE ALL, HEAR ALL

Check out the back cover of this book, and you'll see the Spy University motto: *See all, hear all, know all*. Wouldn't it be nice to see, hear, and know *all* (or at least *more*)? Well, guess what? That's what this guide to **surveillance** is all about! By the time you're through with this month's training, you'll have a whole new set of ways to *see* and *hear* the secrets you want to *know*. You'll be able to:

Disguise a camera so you can secretly take pictures.

Team up with other spies to follow someone, using special hand signals to communicate.

Build a **periscope** to scope out a situation without being seen.

See a *whole* lot through a tiny peephole.

Listen through walls, under doors, and from far away (with some help from your Spy Ear listening device).

As you can *see*, there's a lot of watching and listening in store for you this month, so you'd better sharpen your eyes and clean out your ears! But before we get started, let's clear up a few things by answering some key surveillance questions.

KNOW ALL!

WHAT IS SURVEILLANCE?

Surveillance is the careful study of a **target**. The target can be a person, a place (like a building or a park), or a thing (like a vault full of top secret information). Surveillance can be *visual* or *audio*—that is, it can be done by *eye* or by *ear*.

WHO USES SURVEILLANCE?

Spies, of course, use surveillance to watch and listen (and to tell if they're being watched). **Counterspies** also use surveillance to *catch* spies.

But surveillance is also used outside the spy world. In fact, *you're* probably under surveillance lots of times in your everyday life. When you walk into a store, for example, you're usually under surveillance. There may be security guards, video cameras, or even undercover store detectives (disguised as shoppers) who keep watch over the store to prevent shoplifting. When you enter a bank, you may be watched by a guard and videotaped as part of the bank's efforts to stop bank robbers. When you visit a web site on the Internet, your actions can be monitored and the visit recorded.

WHAT KINDS OF TECHNOLOGY HELP WITH SURVEILLANCE?

Technology plays a huge part in keeping surveillance secret. Spies can use devices like telescopes and binoculars to conduct visual surveillance from a safe distance, and periscopes are good for keeping watch from a hiding place. Cameras are also very useful for visual surveillance, since they create a record of the people, places, things, and events that the spy has observed. On closer inspection, the photos might reveal something that the spy didn't notice while out on the mission.

As for audio surveillance, there's a whole range of listening devices to help spies hear and record conversations from far away. Tiny devices called **bugs** can be hidden in rooms (in walls, furniture, telephones, lamps, electrical plugs—you name it!). These bugs transmit sound from the room to spies at a **listening post** a safe distance away.

IS IT RIGHT TO SECRETLY WATCH PEOPLE AND LISTEN IN ON THEIR CONVERSATIONS?

You may feel funny about watching people, listening to their conversations, or following them around town. That's because you might think that people have a right to privacy. Well, those feelings are understandable. Sometimes surveillance is okay, and sometimes it's not. It all depends on how and why it's done.

During surveillance, you might take part in a conversation and get some useful information just by paying close attention. That's okay, and it's legal, since everyone involved in the conversation knows you're listening. But if you **eavesdrop** (secretly listen to a private conversation), you could be doing something wrong. When two people talk in private, such as on the phone or in a closed room, they don't expect anyone to be listening. So if you *do* listen, you're not respecting their right to privacy. That's why **counterintelligence** officers (counterspies) have to be careful—they can't *legally* listen in on a conversation, even if it's between two suspected spies, unless they go to a judge and get special permission (called a **warrant**). Counterspies have to follow these rules carefully, since they're government employees and have to abide by the law.

Spies, however, don't play by these rules. Breaking them is part of their job description, in fact! But that doesn't mean that *you* should do that. You should stick to the rules, and only use your surveillance techniques with people who know what you're up to (because you've talked to them about it). Make sure they don't mind being involved in your spy training!

ABOUT THIS MONTH'S SPY GEAR

This month you've been issued a see-all, hear-all Surveillance Kit that includes:

■ **A spy mini-camera.** It uses 110-mm film, which can be found at photo shops, supermarkets, or anywhere else film is sold. So, grab some film and start your photography training with **Operation Mini-Cam** on page 10.

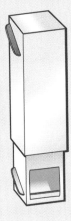

■ **A make-your-own periscope set.** Turn to **Operation Scope It Out** on page 18 for the scoop on this.

■ **A marble to make a wide-angle lens.** Use a marble to make your own version of a high-tech spy device in **Operation Wide Angle** on page 21.

■ **A listening device called a Spy Ear.** *Hear* all about it in **Operation Listen Up!** on page 34.

Store Your Gear!

Your mini-camera and your Spy Ear will fit in these spots in your Spy Case.

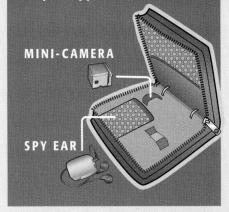

MINI-CAMERA

SPY EAR

ABOUT THIS MONTH'S WEB SITE

Your surveillance training continues on the Spy University web site at **www.scholastic.com/spy**. You can practice tailing an enemy agent, and you can fine-tune your watching and listening skills with more surveillance challenges—like spotting spies on video, and tapping into secret spy conversations! So stop by, and make sure to bring along your new password!

the password spot

This month's web site password:

seehear

A word to wise spies on surveillance missions

■ Always ask permission when you take someone's photo. Some people don't like to have their pictures taken, so ask before you snap.

■ Don't eavesdrop on private conversations.

■ When you practice tailing someone, always ask permission first. If you don't, the person you're following might get upset or annoyed, and you don't want that!

■ Practice your tailing skills at school or in another safe location. Never wander around alone.

■ Do these activities with your friends and family. Recruit a senior spy (an adult) when the mission requires. Good spies and counterspies always operate safely!

Here are this month's spy terms. They appear in **boldface** throughout the book, so you can always turn back to this page to check their meanings.

▼ **Bug:** A miniature listening device that can transmit conversations taking place in a room to a receiver outside the room.

▼ **Camouflage:** To disguise something by making it blend with its surroundings.

▼ **Code:** A system designed to hide the meaning of a message by using letters, numbers, words, symbols, sounds, or signals to represent the actual text.

▼ **Concealment:** A hiding place (for a camera, documents, film, or other spy materials) designed to look like an ordinary object.

▼ **Counterintelligence:** The protection of information, people, and equipment from spies.

▼ **Counterspy:** Someone who works in counterintelligence, investigating and catching spies.

▼ **Eavesdrop:** To secretly listen to a private conversation.

▼ **Espionage:** The field of spying.

▼ **Eye:** The front person in a "Follow the Rabbit" team who has the "Rabbit" in sight during a tailing operation. (See page 26.)

▼ **Instinctive photography:** Taking pictures without looking through a viewfinder.

▼ **Listening post:** A site where audio surveillance is monitored.

▼ **Mole:** An employee of an intelligence service who secretly works for another country's intelligence service.

▼ **Periscope:** A device that allows the user to view areas above, below, behind, or beside him.

▼ **Rabbit:** The person (or target) who's being followed during a tailing operation. (See page 26.)

▼ **Spy network:** A group of spies who work together toward a common goal.

▼ **Surveillance:** The careful study of someone or something.

▼ **Tail:** To follow someone. Can be done by one person, but most often by a team (in which case the rear person is called the "Tail").

▼ **Target:** A person, a place, or a thing that is the object of surveillance.

▼ **Tradecraft:** The set of techniques and procedures spies use to do their work.

▼ **Warrant:** A document, given by the courts, that lets a counterspy (or police agency) do something that would otherwise be against the law (like listening to a private telephone conversation).

The STASI (the East German Security Service) hid a surveillance camera inside this eyeglass case. There aren't *really* any glasses inside. The STASI just made it *look* that way by attaching the edges of a pair of eyeglasses to the case.

LENS OPENING

PARTS OF A PAIR OF GLASSES

THE SEARCH FOR THE DIGGER

The school bell rings, and you're out the door to meet your friends. It's Wednesday, and the week is half over, so on the way home you make plans for the weekend. It's never too early to start thinking about what you can do with your free time!

As you arrive at your house, you see that your next-door neighbor, Mrs. Tulley, is on the front porch talking to your mom. You hear her say, "I'm sure it was your dog. Who else would dig up my flowers? I always see him in my yard."

"But Ringo's not a digger," your mother replies. "I'm sure there's another explanation."

"Not as far as I'm concerned," Mrs. Tulley says. "I'm having the garden society over to my house next weekend, and my yard has to be perfect. I'm running for society president, you know, and I can't have dogs digging up my flowers!"

"Well," your mother replies, "we'll keep Ringo on his chain or in the house, just in case. But I really don't think it's him."

Mrs. Tulley nods, turns, and walks down the sidewalk toward her house.

"You can't keep Ringo tied up!" you say to your mom. "He hates that! He likes to run free. Besides, he would *never* dig up Mrs. Tulley's flowers. She's wrong, and I'm going to prove it."

You run into the house and up to your room. You've got to find out who (or what) dug up Mrs. Tulley's garden. But how are you going to do that?

- If you decide to call a meeting of your spy network to ask for help, turn to **page 12.**

- If you decide to find out what happened to Mrs. Tulley's garden on your own, turn to **page 17.**

This is your Spy Quest for this month. There's only one way to solve it, so choose your path wisely! If you hit a dead end, you'll have to back up and choose another path!

#1 Mini-Cam

SPYmissions

C ameras are ever so important in **surveillance**—and the tinier they are, the better. That way, they can be hidden in the palm of your hand, tucked into a hiding place, and packed easily in your Spy Case with the rest of your Spy Gear. Your mini-camera has an especially compact design, thanks to the 110-mm film it uses. It's different in other ways from bigger, bulkier, every-day cameras, too. So, since spies need to know their gear inside and out, try this activity to see exactly what your mini-camera can do.

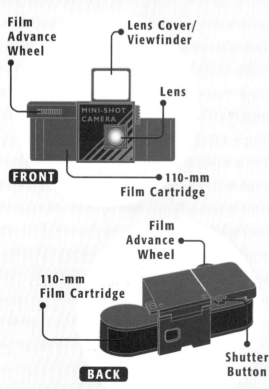

Film Advance Wheel

Lens Cover/ Viewfinder

Lens

MINI-SHOT CAMERA

FRONT

110-mm Film Cartridge

Film Advance Wheel

110-mm Film Cartridge

Shutter Button

BACK

WHAT YOU DO

1 Load the 110-mm film cartridge into the camera. To do this, lift the flaps on the back and right side of the camera and insert the film cartridge upside down at the rear of the camera. Then close the rear plastic flap and turn the film advance wheel until it locks. The camera is now ready to take a picture. **See illustration #1 on page 11.**

2 To take a picture, raise the lens cover/view-finder until it clicks into place. **See illustration #2.** When you're not using the camera, lower the lens cover/viewfinder to protect the lens.

3 For your first photo, choose a large, stationary object outside, like a parked car, a sign, a tree, or a mailbox. Hold the camera steady, look through the viewfinder to aim the camera, and press the shutter button gently. Make sure to

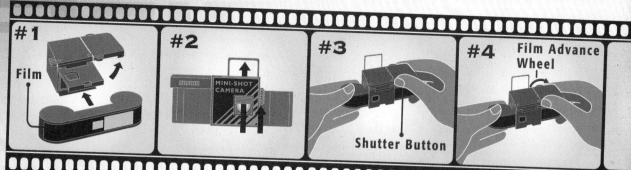

#1 Film
#2 MINI-SHOT CAMERA
#3 Shutter Button
#4 Film Advance Wheel

keep your fingers away from the camera's lens, or your fingertips will be in all of your pictures! **See illustration #3.**

4 To take the next picture, turn the film advance until it locks. **See illustration #4.**

5 Keep a photo log for your first roll of film. For each photo, record the following information:

- The **subject** of your photo (a person, a dog, a house, and so on). Spies use cameras to photograph people, places, events, and things, so try a few pictures of each.

- What the **lighting** was like when you took the picture (sunny, cloudy, inside with bright lights, and so on).

- The **distance** from which you took the picture (3 feet [1 m], 10 feet [3 m], long distance, and so on).

- Whether the object was **moving** when you took the picture.

	Subject	Lighting	Distance	Moving?
1	mailbox	sunny	5 feet	no
2	car	sunny	10 feet	yes
3	house	cloudy	long distance	no
4	cat	inside with bright lights	3 feet	no
5	brother	inside with bright lights	5 feet	no

Later, when you get your developed photos back, you can see which conditions resulted in the best pictures.

6 After you've taken photos with the entire roll of film, turn the film advance wheel as far as it goes, open the back of the camera, and remove the film. Take the film to a photo shop to have the pictures developed. How do you like your photos? Which ones turned out the best?

MORE FROM HEADQUARTERS

Try the techniques described in the next two operations (**Operation Sneaky Shot** and **Operation Camera Camouflage**) to get an even better idea of what your camera can do. Then you can get all your experimenting done on one roll of film!

WHAT'S THE SECRET?

To take good photos with a mini-camera, you'll need practice, a steady hand, and plenty of light. You'll most likely get the best results outside on a sunny day, and your best pictures will probably be of stationary objects that are about 10 feet (3 m) away from you. If you try to take a picture of an object that's closer than 3 feet (1 m) or moving fast, the image will be blurry.

So, how does this little camera take pictures? Even though it's so tiny, it still has the same basic functions as a regular camera. Turn the page to find out how it works.

This tiny camera (almost as small as a thimble) is built just like your mini-camera, with a film cartridge on the outside to keep the camera small. East German spies used this camera to photograph documents in the late 1950s.

HOW THE CAMERA WORKS

The camera's lens focuses the light that reflects off of an object, such as a person or a tree. The lens will focus the light onto the film, where a chemical reaction creates an image. Once the film is developed, the image becomes visible as a negative (those brown strips that come back from the developer with your photos), with dark areas appearing light and light areas appearing dark. Then, when the image is printed, the developer's light shines through the negative, casting the image onto light-sensitive photo paper. The paper has a special way of catching the light, using different layers for different colors, to make the image look like real life again.

SPYtales

In the 1820s, J. N. Niepce used a lens to project an image onto light-sensitive paper, creating the first photographic camera (in a basic sense). That process was improved in the late 1830s, when the French inventor Louis J. M. Daguerre developed the light-sensitive daguerreotype, a photographic plate on which an image could be permanently recorded. With this invention, photography got its real start. It wasn't long before the camera found its way into the spy world. As you might remember reading in your *Trainee Handbook*, cameras were sent up in gas balloons during the American Civil War (1861–1865) to photograph military forces!

SPYquest

(continued from page 9)

You call a meeting of your spy network, Spy Force One. They all arrive in less than half an hour, so there's still plenty of time to come up with a plan before everyone has to go home for dinner.

Lots of ideas get tossed around. Jeff wants to set up an observation post to keep an eye on Mrs. Tulley's garden. Liz thinks that may take too long, and besides, maybe the digging is being done at night. Sam thinks that maybe you should make a list of all the dogs in the neighborhood that could have done the digging. At least that's a start. Sarah still isn't convinced that Ringo is innocent, so she thinks Ringo should be on the list, too. Zoe thinks that everyone should keep their eyes and ears open at school. Maybe someone has seen another dog digging up other yards in the neighborhood.

You wonder which of these ideas will get your investigation off to the right start, and which of them will just lead to dead ends....

- If you decide to set up an observation post at home, turn to page 20.
- If you decide to make a list of other dogs that could have done the digging, turn to **page 22.**
- If you decide to do some listening at school, turn to **page 31.**

OPERATION Sneaky SHOT

As a spy, you never want to be seen "spying." Remember rule number one of being a spy: Don't draw attention to yourself. That's not so simple, though, when you have to take photos, since cameras attract a *lot* of attention. Also, in many places where security is tight, photography is forbidden. So, spies have to be sneaky about their camera work. They learn the techniques of **instinctive photography** (taking pictures without looking through the camera's viewfinder) and other ways of being secretive about their photo-snapping. This operation will introduce you to those skills, so grab your camera (and make it *snappy*!).

STUFF YOU'LL NEED

- ⊙⊙ **Mini-camera**
- **Film cartridge (110 mm)**
- **Notebook**
- **Pencil**

YOUR NETWORK

- **A friend you can photograph**

  Note: It's best to do this activity outside on a sunny day.

WHAT YOU DO

METHOD 1: BASIC INSTINCT

When it would be too obvious to lift a camera to your eye, it's time for instinctive photography. Follow these steps to see how it's done.

1 Hold the camera in your right hand so that your thumb is on the shutter button and the lens of the camera is pointing away from your palm. The lens cover should be raised.

2 Hold your right arm by your side.

3 To take a picture, simply rotate your hand until the camera is pointing in the right direction and click the shutter. Don't look down at your hand. People will look where you look, so keep your eyes off your camera!

4 Casually turn your arm back to its original position.

5 Take several pictures of stationary objects (or of a friend who's standing still). Practice holding the camera slightly up or down at different angles so that you can photograph things that are closer to the ground or higher in the air. Keep a log describing how you were holding the camera for each picture. When you have the film developed, you'll see how well you aimed the camera by instinct. Practice will help!

METHOD 2: FROM OUT OF NOWHERE

Try this method to see how a tree can play a part in sneaky shots.

1 Find a tree that's big enough for you to stand behind, and have a friend stand several feet away from it.

2 Again, hold the camera in your right hand so that your thumb is on the shutter button and the lens of the camera is pointing away from your palm. Make sure that the lens cover is raised.

3 Stick your right arm out with the lens of the camera pointing at your friend. Only your wrist,

hand, and camera should be visible on the other side of the tree.

4 To make sure your arm doesn't wobble (which would give you a blurry picture!), brace your arm against the tree.

5 Click the shutter, then quickly pull your arm back behind the tree.

This surveillance camera was used by the KGB (the intelligence service of the former Soviet Union) from the 1950s through the 1970s. Spies used it to take photos instinctively while holding the camera secretly in one hand. Pressing the thumb lever would snap a picture and advance the film at the same time.

MORE FROM HEADQUARTERS

Try a variation on Method 2. Rather than hiding behind a tree, practice taking a picture around the corner of a building. Make sure that only your hand and the camera stick out from behind the building.

WHAT'S THE SECRET?

It takes practice to take good pictures without looking through the camera's viewfinder, so give yourself some time. Remember to keep your arm still, and when taking a picture from around a corner or behind a tree, brace yourself!

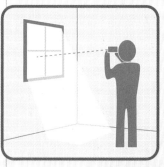

Spies also have a special set of techniques for taking pictures from windows. They stand a few feet back from the window and take the picture from there. That way, they're not standing directly in the light, which would make them visible from outside the window.

I n your *Trainee Handbook*, you learned how to disguise a camera by tucking it into a newspaper. That was just *one* of the many, many ways a camera can be hidden. This operation will show you another option, especially designed for your mini-camera. Try it and see if you can imagine your own methods of clever *cameraflage*!

STUFF YOU'LL NEED

- 👓 **Mini-camera**
- **Film cartridge (110 mm)**
- **Small bag of potato chips**
- **Scissors**
- **Double-sided tape (or loops of regular tape)**
- **Small plastic sandwich bag**

WHAT YOU DO

1 Carefully open the top of the potato chip bag. Remove the chips and set them aside for later.

2 Cut a small hole near the middle of the bag, just the right size for the camera lens. Put a small piece of double-sided tape on either side of the hole (on the inside of the bag). You can also use loops of regular tape if you don't have double-sided tape.

Camera hole

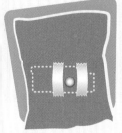

3 Raise the camera's viewfinder to open the lens, and place the camera in the bag, positioning the camera so the lens points out of the hole. Press the camera onto the tape. The tape will hold the camera in place.

4 Fill the small plastic sandwich bag with chips, and tape it to the inside of the bag, on the side opposite the camera. That way, when you're not snapping pictures, you can *really* snack on chips, making your bag seem all the more innocent!

5 Now you're ready to snap a picture. So, aim the camera by pointing the bag in the right direction. Then, holding the bag steady, put your free hand into the bag as if you're reaching for a potato chip. Instead, press the shutter button to snap a picture!

Click!

6 To advance the film, keep your hand inside the bag and turn the advance wheel. You might want to crinkle the bag a bit (or chew on some chips!) while doing this, so no one hears the sound of the turning wheel.

This camera was hidden behind a necktie and took pictures through a glass tie-tack. It was used by the KGB (the intelligence service of the former Soviet Union) in the 1980s.

GLASS TIE-TACK

LENS

REMOTE SHUTTER RELEASE
(HIDDEN IN SPY'S PANTS POCKET)

CAMERA
(USUALLY BEHIND TIE)

Click!

1 If you have an old handkerchief that you can cut a hole in, you can hide a camera underneath it. Just cut an opening for the camera's lens and tape the camera to the cloth. Then hold the handkerchief in your hand as if you have a cold and you need to be ready for your next sneeze!

2 What other disguises can you dream up for your mini-camera? You know the technique now, so get creative!

SPYtales

The *Ministerium für Staatssicherheit* (MfS), known as the STASI, was the East German intelligence and security service from 1950 until 1990, when East and West Germany merged after the fall of the Berlin Wall (and the STASI ceased to exist). From its headquarters in East Berlin, the STASI not only spied on other countries, but it also kept its own citizens under surveillance at home. This was easy for them because lots of people volunteered to be informers (which means they'd report anything they thought was suspicious). In fact, in 1990, the STASI had 173,000 registered informers out of a population of less than 17,000,000. That's one informer for every hundred people!

The STASI was also famous for its use of cameras. Special holes for cameras were drilled into the walls of hotel rooms throughout East Germany, and cameras were concealed in coin purses, handbags, eyeglass cases, umbrellas—just about any spot imaginable. The STASI even had cameras that could take infrared photos (using invisible light) through the side of a briefcase!

INFRARED PHOTO FLASH UNITS

INFRARED CAMER

INFRARED PHOTO FLOOD LIGHT

POWER SUPPLY

FABRIC SIDE TO ALLOW
INFRARED LIGHT THROU

CONCEALED TRIGGER TO TAKE FLASH PHOTOGRAPH

A STASI infrared briefcase camera. The side of the briefcase was made of a special fabric that allowed photos to be taken through it.

WHAT'S THE SECRET?

Tiny cameras are great for disguising. They can hide in lots of small places where larger, everyday cameras can't fit. Who would ever imagine a camera tucked inside a small bag of potato chips? That's the idea here, and that's the idea behind all spy **concealments** (or hiding places) for cameras. The camera should be hidden in a place that no one would ever suspect! Check out the photos on these pages for a few examples of how crafty spies can be!

These days, even tiny *video* cameras can be hidden in places you'd never suspect. Here's one hidden in a baseball cap.

Two microvideo cameras. The one on the left is shown at actual size.

CIRCUIT BOARD

19.069928
MHz
S.H.C

PINHOLE LENSES

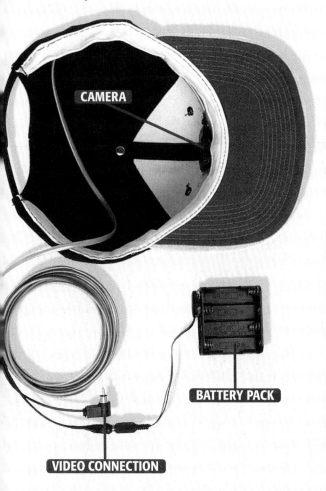

CAMERA

BATTERY PACK

VIDEO CONNECTION

SPYquest

(continued from page 9)

You decide to run this operation by yourself. It may be harder that way, but you think you've got the training to pull it off. The first thing you need is a plan. If Ringo isn't the digger, then could it have been another dog? There are a number of dogs in the neighborhood that could have done the digging, but most are kept on leashes, or chained to a tree or to their doghouses. It seems impossible to set up surveillance on *all* the dogs in the neighborhood, but you could at least look around. Or maybe you could take a close look at Mrs. Tulley's garden to see if the digger left any traces.

- If you decide to look around the neighborhood to see if another dog is running loose, turn to **page 39**.

- If you decide to take a close look at Mrs. Tulley's garden, turn to **page 25**.

#4 Scope It Out

Sometimes it's tough to watch a **target** without being seen, especially if you're in a hiding place and you don't want to poke your head out. That's when a special device called a **periscope** comes in handy. This operation will show you how to build one, using the cardboard tubes and mirrors in this month's Spy Gear kit. When you're done, you'll be able to see above you, below you, around corners, and even *behind* you, without giving up your hiding place (or even turning your head)!

WHAT YOU DO

PART 1: MAKING THE PERISCOPE

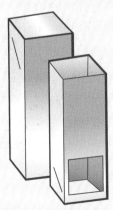

1 Squeeze the opposite edges of the cardboard sleeves to make them into two rectangular tubes. You'll notice that one is larger than the other and has a flap on top. Close that flap.

2 Slide the smaller tube inside the larger tube. The rectangular view holes should be on opposite ends and opposite sides.

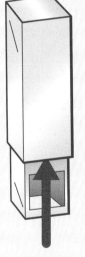

3 Peel off the protective plastic from the two mirrors and slide the mirrors into the slots on each end of the long tube. The shiny sides of the mirrors need to be facing each other. Tape the mirrors to the tubes to hold them in place. Make sure the mirrors don't bend at all, or you'll have a lot of trouble seeing reflections in them!

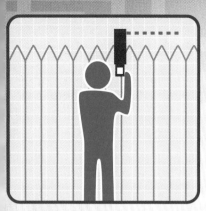

4 Hold your periscope upright and look into the bottom view hole. You'll be able to see *above* you. Won't this be handy for looking over fences? (And if you flip the periscope so the view hole is on top, you can check out what's going on *below* you, too.)

5 Now hold the tube horizontally and look into the view hole. This is the way you would position the periscope if you wanted to see *around a corner*.

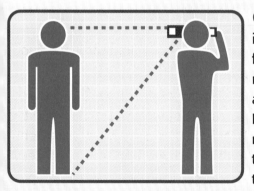

6 Now it's time for some rearview action! First, remove the small tube and turn it so that its view hole faces the same direction as the larger tube's view hole. Slide the small tube into place. Hold the periscope horizontally and look through the bottom view hole. Now you have eyes in the back of your head!

7 When you're ready to take your periscope out on a mission, choose whichever view you want and tape the tubes in place (so they don't slide!).

PART 2: PERISCOPE IN ACTION!

Now that your periscope is ready for action, it's time to give it some finishing touches and take it on a test run. For this part, you'll need some family members or friends who are willing to be watched. Let them know that you'll be watching them at some point during the day with your latest spy gadget (but don't tell them exactly what it is!). Challenge them to catch you watching!

1 The first step is to choose a hiding place. Think of a spot where you'll be able to scope out your target (or targets), either inside or outside.

2 The picture below shows you ways you can **camouflage** your periscope to blend in with your hiding place. For example, if you plan to be inside peeking around a white wall, then your periscope is already the right color. However, if you want to go outside and hide around bushes or trees, you might want to cover your periscope with brown or green paper (or paint it) and glue leaves to it. If you're going to be observing from a shadowy place, you could cover your periscope with black paper. It's up to you.

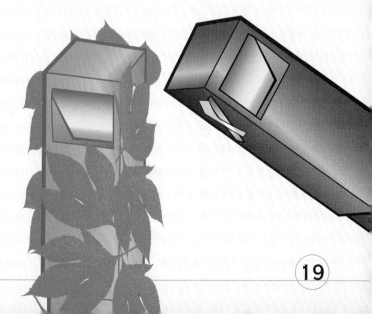

3 Once you've chosen a good location and prepared your periscope to match it, it's time to start your **surveillance**. So, get yourself set up in your hiding place, extend your periscope, and see how long you can watch before your target catches on. If your target *does* see you, ask what gave you away. If your target *never* sees you, just finish when you've had enough and let your target know you were successful (without bragging *too* much) by sharing what you observed!

MORE FROM HEADQUARTERS

Try other hiding places, and see which ones allow you to watch for the longest times—or maybe without ever being seen at all! You'll be most successful if you keep really still and quiet. You'll probably also find that it's best to stay low to the ground, so your periscope won't easily catch your target's eye.

WHAT'S THE SECRET?

Your periscope works because of its two mirrors. Mirrors reflect light. The image you see bounces off one mirror, is reflected to the other, and then bounces off the second mirror, out the view hole, and into your eye. Your periscope gives you a view of whatever area the top mirror is facing.

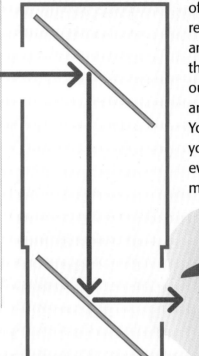

SPYquest

(continued from page 12)

The observation post seems like a good idea. Fortunately, you have a great view of Mrs. Tulley's garden from your bedroom window, so you agree to take the first watch. You get out your notebook so you can record your observations.

The first thing you see is Mrs. Tulley working to fill the hole in her garden. She carefully replaces the plants that were destroyed and smoothes the dirt. You notice that she's talking to herself—or maybe she's talking to her cat, who's watching her from a perch in the window. Just then, you see Brad Barker walking by on the sidewalk in front of Mrs. Tulley's house. He stops suddenly, picks up a rock, and throws it at a squirrel in one of Mrs. Tulley's trees. Mrs. Tulley sees this and shouts, "Stop that!"

Brad just looks at her scornfully and keeps walking. Brad Barker is the school bully. He's got a mean streak like you've never seen before, and you

know he has a dog! He's a real suspect, you think. It would be just like him to let his dog dig up someone's garden. But if it *is* Brad's dog, how can you prove it? Should you watch Brad, or should you just keep watching Mrs. Tulley's garden?

■ If you decide to check out Brad tomorrow after school, turn to **page 28**.

■ If you decide to keep up your surveillance on Mrs. Tulley's garden, turn to **page 37**.

OPERATION
#5 WIDE ANGLE

In **Operation Scope It Out**, you created a gadget that's good for seeing around corners, over fences, from behind bushes, and from lots of other hiding places, too. But did you know spies also have special devices that help them see through walls? Well, *almost* through walls. All they need is a tiny hole, and they can see a *whole* lot. Try this activity, and you'll see!

STUFF YOU'LL NEED

- **One sheet of black construction paper (roughly 9 x 12 inches [23 x 30 cm])**
- **Scissors**
- **Ruler**
- **Tape**
- **Clear marble**

WHAT YOU DO

1 Cut the sheet of construction paper in half so you have two pieces that are roughly 9 x 6 inches (23 x 15 cm) each.

2 Roll the paper into a tube that's about ½ inch (1.25 cm) across.

3 Tape the tube to hold it in place.

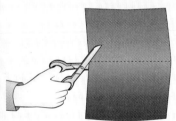

4 Take the other half of the paper and place the marble at one corner.

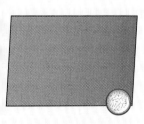

5 Roll the paper into a tube around the marble. The tube should be tight around the marble, and the marble should be placed so that half of it is sticking out the end of the tube.

6 Tape the tube to hold it in place.

7 Stand in the doorway of your room and look through the first tube (without the marble). How much of your room can you see?

8 Now look at your room through the *second* tube with the marble at the opposite end of the tube. How much can you see this time? Do you see why we're going to call your latest spy gadget creation a *wide-angle viewer*?

This camera has a long wide-angle lens that can be placed in a hole drilled in a wall.

MORE FROM HEADQUARTERS

Test the range of your new wide-angle viewer. Have a friend stand about 10 feet (3 m) in front of you. Look at your friend through your viewer. Have her move slowly to the left until you can no longer see her. Have her then move slowly to the right until you can't see her on that side, either. How far can she move and still be seen?

WHAT'S THE SECRET?

Only a little bit of the world outside your window is visible when you look through the first paper tube. But when you look through the tube with the *marble*, you can suddenly see much more. There's a catch, however—what you see is smaller than actual size and *upside down*! That's because the marble is acting like a special kind of lens. A lens is a curved piece of glass or plastic that bends rays of light that pass through it. The light-bending power of this particular lens makes faraway objects appear upside down and smaller than actual size. This means you can see more than you would through a hole the same

size as the marble (since everything's so tiny, more fits in the space!).

The wide-angle viewer you built is similar to a device that spies use. If a spy wants to watch people in the next room, he'll first drill a very small hole in the wall between the rooms. The hole is sometimes no wider than the lead in a pencil and is not easily seen (especially by the people who are being watched). The spy then takes a thin tube with a wide-angle lens at one end and sticks it through the hole. The lens lets the spy see the entire room. In most situations, the spy will connect the lens to a video camera so he can record what's going on.

(continued from page 12)

Your list includes all the dogs in your neighborhood and names of their owners. Two names jump out. One is Brad Barker, the school bully. He has an English bulldog that you've seen on his porch. You can imagine Brad's dog destroying a garden. You can even imagine Brad *encouraging* that kind of thing!

Then there's Jennifer Caponi. You've heard something about Jennifer's dog being a real jumper. Maybe the dog sometimes jumps over Jennifer's fence and roams the neighborhood in search of gardens to dig up?

- If you decide to investigate Brad and his dog, turn to **page 28**.
- If you decide to check out Jennifer and her dog, turn to **page 33**.

OPERATION MOVING Target

Now it's time to learn a key **surveillance** skill: how to **tail** someone. Just like it sounds, when you tail a person (who's called your **target**), you're trailing behind him. You're following his every move, but you're keeping yourself out of view. It's not easy, but it's an important way to collect information. **Counterspies** will often tail a suspected spy in order to find out more about his habits and routines. Although this information may seem unimportant at first, it often leads to more valuable information later. For example, a suspect's walk through a crowded park every day may mean that he's dropping off secret information there.

So, find a friend who's willing to be your target (sometimes called "the customer" by counterspies), and let's get *moving!*

STUFF YOU'LL NEED

- **Notebook**
- **Pencil**
- **Watch**
- **Quick disguises (sunglasses, jacket, hat)**
- **Backpack**

YOUR NETWORK

- **A friend who's willing to be your target**

WHAT YOU DO

Can you learn something new about your friend by following him for half an hour? Follow these steps to see what you can find out!

1 Gather several friends together. Tell them that during the next week, you're going to tail one of them. Don't tell them who you're going to follow.

2 Choose the friend you'll follow. He'll be your target. Next, choose a time and a place to tail your target. Remember that you should follow your friend in a safe location, so if you have some free time at school (like at lunch or recess), that's a good choice. In this operation, you'll tail your target for half an hour.

A word to wise spies

Tail your friend at school or in another safe location.

3 Use a notebook to create a surveillance log. On the left side, create a blank chart where you can record what you see. On the right side, leave a blank space where you can draw a map, if necessary. Your surveillance log could look like the one at the bottom of this page.

4 Check out the list of Tailing Tips on the next page to prepare for your mission. As you learned in your *Trainee Handbook*, it'll help to have a jacket or a hat available for a quick change of appearance. Sunglasses are a good idea, too. So, pack your backpack accordingly.

5 When the time comes, find your target and get on his tail. Remember, you have to stay close enough to the target to make sure he doesn't give you the slip, but far enough away that he won't realize you're there. Make notes whenever you have a spare moment.

6 After tailing your target for half an hour, review your notes. Answer the following questions:

- **Is there anything the target did that surprised you?**

- **Could you guess what was being said when the target talked to people?**

- **Did the target realize you were tailing him?**

- **Did you learn something new about your friend?**

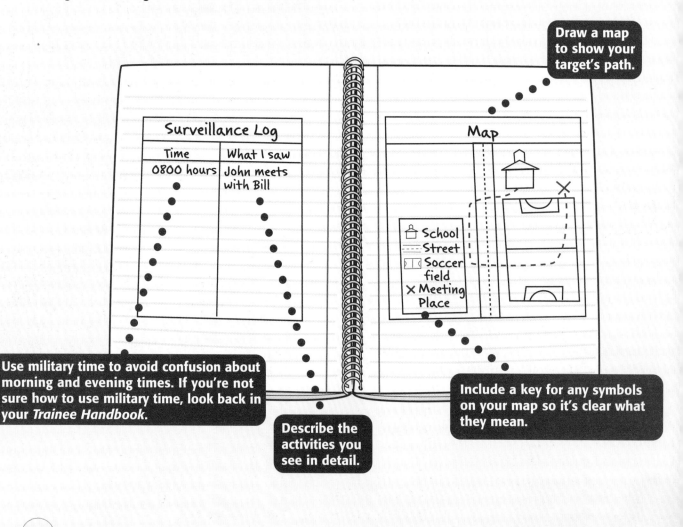

Draw a map to show your target's path.

Surveillance Log

Time	What I saw
0800 hours	John meets with Bill

Map

School
Street
Soccer field
✕ Meeting Place

Use military time to avoid confusion about morning and evening times. If you're not sure how to use military time, look back in your *Trainee Handbook*.

Describe the activities you see in detail.

Include a key for any symbols on your map so it's clear what they mean.

MORE FROM HEADQUARTERS

Visit the Spy University web site at **www.scholastic.com/spy** to test your tailing skills! You can also watch a surveillance video and use your eagle eyes to spot some spies!

WHAT'S THE SECRET?

It's not easy to tail a person without being noticed. You may think that your task was doubly difficult because the person you were following knew you and knew you might follow him. But real-life counterspies don't have it any easier! Spies always suspect they're being followed. It's this kind of caution that keeps the spy alive and his role as a spy a secret.

Tailing can be a lot more successful when it's done by a team. The next operation will show you how that's done, so read on!

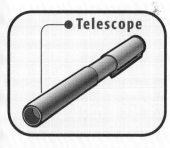

● **Telescope**

Your Telemicro (from your Trainee Kit) is good to have along on tailing operations, so you can keep watch from afar.

Tailing Tips

■ Never make eye contact with your target.

■ Wear sunglasses (but only if it's a sunny day!) so you can watch your target without being obvious. The sunglasses are also a form of disguise.

■ Be prepared to change your appearance to keep your target from recognizing you. Carry a jacket or a hat (or both) to provide a quick disguise.

■ If your target stops suddenly, you shouldn't stop suddenly, too! Your target may be testing to see if you're following him. If you stop suddenly, you'll confirm his suspicions! So, keep moving, and resume your tail later (after a quick change!).

■ Take cover when necessary (but only when it looks natural)! Move into a crowd, turn away, or cover your face (without being obvious) if you think your target might be looking your way.

SPYquest

(continued from page 17)

You look around Mrs. Tulley's yard to see if anyone's watching. The coast is clear, except for the cat that's watching you from the window. You examine the garden. There's a hole, all right, with dirt spread everywhere and a couple of plants that have been destroyed by the digging. You look around the dirt for any signs of dog prints, but there are none. You kneel down to get a closer look, but then you hear:

"Please get out of my garden!" You look up to see Mrs. Tulley coming toward you with a wheelbarrow full of plants.

"Sorry," you say, rising to your feet. "I was just checking to see if there were any dog prints in the dirt. I didn't see any."

"I've already moved the dirt around, that's why!" she insists.

"But did you see any dog prints

before?" you ask.

"If you're trying to prove something, don't bother," she says. "The answer to this problem is simple: *Your* dog needs to be kept in *your* yard. Period. Now please leave my garden alone—it's enough of a disaster as it is."

■ Oh, well. That didn't prove anything. Go back and see if another path will lead to more answers.

OPERATION FOLLOW THE Rabbit

No, this isn't Wonderland, and you're not supposed to follow the rabbit into a hole in the ground like Alice did! "Follow the Rabbit" is the name for a special spy **tailing** method that involves a team of two people who work together to keep a **target** under watch. The first person is called the **Eye**, because he follows closest to the target and keeps him in view. The second person, called the **Tail**, stays *behind* the Eye. The name for the target in this maneuver is—you guessed it—the **Rabbit**. So, if you're ready to follow a Rabbit, *follow* the instructions below!

STUFF YOU'LL NEED

- **Notebook**
- **Pencil**
- **Watch**
- **Disguises like jackets, hats, and sunglasses (for each tailing team member)**
- **Small backpacks (for each tailing team member)**

YOUR NETWORK

- **A friend to be the Rabbit**
- **A friend to be your tailing teammate**

WHAT YOU DO

Tell several friends that you're going to follow one of them at some point during the week. Later, meet with your tailing teammate and decide who you're going to tail, along with when, where, and how you're going to do it. Your goal should be to learn at least one new thing about your Rabbit!

1 First, you'll have to decide who will be the Eye and who will be the Tail in your "Follow the Rabbit" maneuver.

2 Next, learn the following system of hand signals to communicate during the operation. Since the Eye has the view of the Rabbit, he sends information about the Rabbit's movements back to the Tail. All of these signals were designed (by real spies) to be visible from behind.

A. When the Eye has the Rabbit in sight, he points to the side of his eye to start the surveillance.

RIGHT TURN | **LEFT TURN**

B. If the Rabbit is turning right, the Eye touches his right ear. For a left turn, the Eye touches his left ear.

C. If the Eye puts his hand to his side and turns his palm so that it faces behind him (toward the Tail), then the Rabbit has stopped.

D. If the Eye makes a fist out of his hand at his side, the Rabbit is moving again.

E. If the Eye loses sight of the Rabbit, he rubs the back of his head. This tells the Tail to look around and see if he can find the Rabbit.

3 The Eye and the Tail have to be prepared to swap roles. For example, if the Rabbit stops suddenly, the Eye risks being noticed if he stops suddenly, too. So, when the Eye signals that the Rabbit has stopped, the Tail should also stop. The Eye should keep walking past the Rabbit and wait farther down the street. When the Rabbit continues, the Tail takes over the role of the Eye. The former Eye, waiting down the street, takes over the Tail position after the Rabbit and the Eye pass him.

4 Review the Tailing Tips on page 25 before you start to follow your Rabbit. Be sure you're prepared with a bag of quick disguises if you need to change your appearance in a pinch.

5 Tail your friend using the "Follow the Rabbit" method for half an hour, again keeping a surveillance log. What new things did you find out about the Rabbit?

MORE FROM HEADQUARTERS

1 See if you can develop more hand signals to communicate other instructions to your tailing teammate. Skip ahead to **Operation Give Me a Sign** on page 42 for some ideas.

2 Make sure to stop by the Spy University web site at **www.scholastic.com/spy** for an on-line tailing challenge!

WHAT'S THE SECRET?

If an enemy spy notices the same person, especially a stranger, over and over again, it seems unusual, and he gets suspicious. He automatically becomes more cautious and his movements will become more difficult to track. That's why **counterspies** use teams to follow enemy agents.

One counterspy will follow the enemy spy for a short time, then a second, third, or even a *fourth* counterspy will pick up the tail. Since the enemy spy doesn't see the same person behind him all the time, there's less of a chance that he'll realize he's being followed.

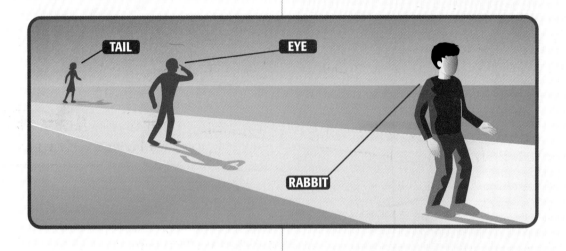

(continued from pages 20, 22, or 31)

You decide to set up surveillance on Brad after school. Liz, a fellow Spy Force One member, agrees to team up with you to do the "Follow the Rabbit" tailing maneuver. Liz will be the Eye, and you'll be the Tail.

Brad is tough to follow. He stops quite a few times, so Liz has to walk past him, making you the Eye, while Liz becomes the Tail. You swap roles many times. But no matter what Brad does, you stay on his tail, and he never notices!

When Brad reaches home, you watch from behind a tree as he walks past his dog, which is chained up on the porch. The dog barks at him, and Brad says, in a nasty tone, "Oh, shut up!"

Brad goes inside, and you decide to stay and watch for a few minutes to see if he comes back out. A few minutes later, Brad's little sister, Emily, arrives home and the dog starts whimpering. Emily unchains the dog, attaches a leash, and starts to walk the dog down the street.

"Maybe we should ask Emily if she thinks her dog could have gotten into Mrs. Tulley's garden?" you suggest.

"Good idea," Liz says.

You approach Emily and ask your question.

"It's not possible," she says. "We never take Wilma off her chain except to walk her, and I'm the only one who ever does that," she says.

"Brad never walks her?" you ask.

"Oh, no. Brad's way too lazy for that. And besides, Wilma *hates* Brad. He throws rocks at her and things," she says.

You and Liz look at each other. It seems pretty clear now that you've been barking up the wrong tree....

■ This is a dead end. Turn back and try another path!

OPERATION STAY Tuned

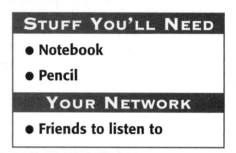

L istening is something that we all do, but we don't always do it well. Your parents may even complain that sometimes you don't listen. But a spy needs to be a good listener—a *great* listener, in fact! When you're a great listener, you really make an effort to hear, understand, and remember what people are saying. So, how great of a listener are you? Are you always ready to absorb information, or do you think there are times when you're just not tuned in? Try this operation to see how much you can hear when you put your mind—and your *ears*—to it!

STUFF YOU'LL NEED
- **Notebook**
- **Pencil**

YOUR NETWORK
- **Friends to listen to**

WHAT YOU DO

A spy can pick up all kinds of interesting information just by hanging around wherever people usually gather and talk. There's no need to be secretive about it—just pick a good place, stick around, and listen! Your goal for this operation is to find out at least five new things about your school, your teachers, or your friends, just by listening for half an hour!

1 Select a time and a place at school where you can listen for half an hour. It should be a place where a lot of people are gathered around, having conversations. You could try hanging around the school office before school starts, or you might try the cafeteria at lunchtime.

2 Go to your location at the selected time and listen! You can answer people who talk to you, but don't start a conversation. Keep any conversations short, and focus on listening instead of talking. Remember that when you're talking, you're not listening (and when you're not listening, you're not learning anything new!).

3 Keep a **surveillance** log to record what you hear. Make sure to note the time when you hear something. Remember that spy operations use military time (look back at your *Trainee Handbook* for a refresher on that). Your surveillance log could look like the example below.

It may seem strange to people if you write in your notebook while you're listening to them, so make your log entries only when it's safe and no one is looking at you. You might also want to disguise your surveillance log as a math note-book, so that from the outside it looks like you're doing your math homework!

4 Review your log at the end of the day. What did you learn that you didn't know before? Did you hear any sounds that you didn't notice before?

5 Repeat the activity on another day, but try a different location and time. Which location was best for gathering information? Which time?

MORE FROM HEADQUARTERS

1 Have several friends each set up a different listening area in the school at the same time. At the end of the day, compile a list of everything that was learned.

2 At home, where would be the best place to set up a listening area? Where does your family get together to talk? At what time would you hear the most?

WHAT'S THE SECRET?

When you don't talk, you hear more. It sounds so easy, but it's not. Listening is a skill that you can learn, just like riding a bike or shooting a jump shot in basketball. It just takes practice.

You also probably learned that *where* you listen affects the kind of information you get. A good spy knows the best places to listen. Spies around the world know that people from different

Location: Outside the front office
Date: November 14

Time	WHAT I HEARD
0830 hours	Mr. Thornton arrives and talks to me. He likes my new gym shoes. He tells me that he played basketball when he was in college. I didn't know that! Cool.
0840 hours	There is a strange humming sound that just started. I haven't heard it before. I'm not sure what it is, but it seems to be coming from behind the door next to the office.
0845 hours	The Sparks twins stop by to tell me they saw Jeff and Maria holding hands on the way to school. Something is definitely up there.
0850 hours	Mrs. Kyle brings Brandon's lunch to school. She tells the secretary that he forgot it at home.

cultures talk in different rooms. For example, Italians and Russians often talk in kitchens, while Americans often talk in family rooms or bedrooms. Is there a special room or part of the house where your family gathers to chat?

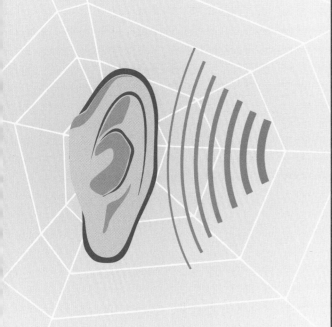

(continued from page 12)

The next morning, Spy Force One is on the job, spread throughout the school, looking around, talking to class-mates, and listening for clues. Liz takes the cafeteria, Sam takes the library, Jeff sits in the hall outside the office, and you head for the gym.

You meet at lunch to discuss what everyone has found out. It's amazing what's going on at school. Jennifer told Liz that her brother has poison ivy all over his body, and Yoshi told Sam that his father is taking him on a trip to Peru. But Jeff comes up with the most useful news. Brad Barker, the school bully, was called into the principal's office before school. When he came out, he muttered something to him-self (which was overheard by everyone around him) about getting his dog to bite the principal! That makes you wonder: Would he have had his dog dig up Mrs. Tulley's garden? Maybe Mrs. Tulley made him mad at some point?

■ If you decide to ask Mrs. Tulley if she's ever had a problem with Brad, turn to **page 35.**

■ If you decide to set up surveillance on Brad after school, turn to **page 28.**

SPYtales

Patience Wright may have been the first woman spy for the United States. During the American Revolutionary War (1775-1783), Wright lived in London, England, and worked as a sculptor. She was well known, and important British people, including military personnel, came to her studio to have their heads sculpted out of wax. While she sculpted, Wright charmed her subjects into talking about a wide range of topics, including military and political matters. But this was not just polite conversation! Wright was carefully steering her subjects to these topics for a reason. She was spying for the American Continental Army, collecting information and sending it to America inside of wax heads!

Unfortunately, though, it appears that the British found out about Wright's espionage, so they made sure that the information she provided to the Americans was useless in the end.

OPERATION Talking WALLS

If walls could talk, it would sure make a spy's job easier, since lots of secrets are discussed behind closed doors. But walls *don't* talk, so a spy needs other tricks to hear what's going on in the next room. And *no*, you don't need a special high-tech gadget. You just need to know a little about walls and a bit about the way sound travels, and you'll have your walls sharing secrets in no time!

STUFF YOU'LL NEED

- **TV set or radio**
- **Drinking glass**

WHAT YOU DO

1 Switch on the TV or radio in one room. Turn the sound to a medium level.

2 Go to the room next door and close the door behind you. How well can you hear the sound of the TV or radio now? It should be very soft. If it's not, go turn the TV or radio down a little bit.

3 Place the opening of the drinking glass against the wall that separates the room you're in from the room with the TV or radio. Can you hear more now?

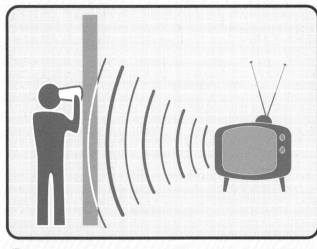

4 Move the glass slowly across the wall. Are there places in the wall where the sound from the other room is louder or clearer?

MORE FROM HEADQUARTERS

1 Ask some friends to carry on a conversation in the room next door. With a drinking glass against the wall, can you hear what they're saying?

 2 Visit the Spy University web site at **www.scholastic.com/spy** and listen to some secret spy conversations. See if you can piece together what's being said before time runs out!

WHAT'S THE SECRET?

Every sound you hear is caused by vibrations. These vibrations travel through the air as *sound waves*. The sound waves from the TV traveled through the air to the wall, causing the wall to vibrate slightly. When you pressed the glass to the wall, the glass amplified those vibrations (or made them louder) so you could hear them.

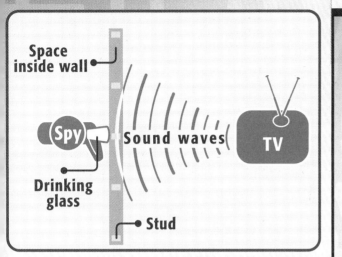

Space inside wall

Spy

Sound waves

TV

Drinking glass

Stud

When you moved the glass around on the wall, you probably noticed that the sound was louder and clearer sometimes. That's because the walls of most houses are hollow except in certain spots, where there are *studs* (solid, vertical wooden or steel pieces that give the wall support). Since sound waves travel better through solids (and liquids) than through air, you'll hear more when you place the glass over a solid wooden or steel stud.

This device, called an "accelerometer," can be used to listen through 1½ foot (.45 m) concrete walls. When the spike is imbedded in the wall, the device will pick up vibrations coming from the other side of the wall and transmit them to a listening post.

SPYquest

(*continued from page 22*)

You head down to Jennifer's house to check out her dog right away. As you're looking around to see if you can spot the dog, Jennifer comes out of the front door. You say hello and ask her where her dog is today. She gives you a funny look and says, "Dog? What dog?"

"Don't you have a dog?" you ask.

She looks puzzled and replies, "Who told you I have a dog? The only pet I have is a rabbit named Thumper."

Guess there's no fence-jumping dog around here!

■ This is a dead end. Go back and choose a different route!

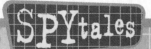

SPYtales

Things had not been going well for the American Continental Army during the early days of the Revolutionary War. The British Army had beaten the Americans in several key battles. But on the night of December 4, 1777, that changed. The British army marched out of Philadelphia for what they thought was a surprise attack on the Continental Army camped eight miles away. But the Americans weren't surprised at all! With cannons ready, they battled the British to a standstill. Two days later, the British army retreated to Philadelphia.

But how did the Americans know about the surprise attack? It was all thanks to Lydia Darragh, a volunteer spy. During the fall of 1777, a group of British officers barged into her home and took over her parlor, which they used as a meeting room. On the night of December 2, Darragh learned of the planned British attack and managed to slip through the British lines and get word to the Americans just in time. Darragh didn't get her information by deciphering a code or intercepting a secret message. She simply hid in a closet that backed onto the parlor and listened through the walls!

Listen Up!

Wouldn't it be great to have superpowered ears so you could hear whispers from across a room? Well, wish no more—it can happen! Just turn on your Spy Ear listening device, point it in the right direction, and those sound waves will be yours! This activity will show you how the Spy Ear works, and then it'll show you how you can make the device even *more* superpowered! So, get ready to catch some sound waves!

STUFF YOU'LL NEED

- **Radio**
- **Spy Ear listening device**
- **Large mixing bowl (as round as possible)**

YOUR NETWORK

- **A friend you can listen to**

WHAT YOU DO

PART 1: I HEARD THAT!

1 Turn the radio on. Set the volume so low that you can barely hear it.

2 Stand about 10 feet (3 m) away. The sound from the radio should be even softer now. Maybe you won't even hear it at all.

3 Place the Spy Ear's earphones in your ears and then plug them into the earphone jack.

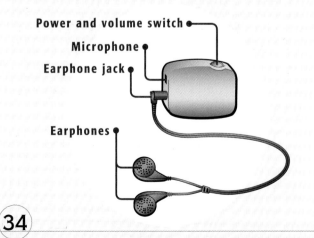

Power and volume switch

Microphone

Earphone jack

Earphones

4 Switch on the Spy Ear and turn the volume to a medium setting.

5 Point the Spy Ear's microphone at the radio. How loud is the radio now?

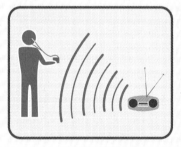

6 Try different volume settings on the Spy Ear and the radio, and try different distances from the radio, too. How far away can you be and still hear the radio?

PART 2: EASY LISTENER

1 Go outside and have a friend walk about 20 feet (6.5 m) away from you and stay there. Have her talk in a normal tone of voice. How well can you hear what she's saying?

2 Again, place the Spy Ear's earphones in your ears, plug them into the earphone jack, switch on the Spy Ear, and turn the volume to a medium setting.

3 Point the Spy Ear's microphone at your friend and again have her talk in a normal tone of voice. How much can you hear this time?

4 Next, hold the bowl in front of you so that the opening of the bowl faces your friend.

5 Hold the Spy Ear's microphone so it faces the inside of the bowl. The device should be in the middle of the bowl, at an equal distance from all sides.

6 Have your friend speak in a normal tone of voice and again listen to what she's saying. How does she sound this time? If she's not any louder, move the Spy Ear in and out of the bowl until you find the spot that gives you the best sound.

MORE FROM HEADQUARTERS

1 Repeat Part 2, only this time hold the microphone at different distances away from the bowl. Is there one place where you can hear the sound best?

2 Try using a larger or smaller bowl. How do those changes affect what you can hear?

3 Make a cone out of a large sheet of paper, leaving an opening at the point of the cone. Place the listening device microphone against the opening on the point of the cone. Does this help your Spy Ear pick up more sound?

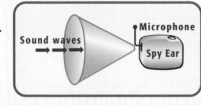

WHAT'S THE SECRET?

Your Spy Ear has a little microphone that picks up sounds and amplifies them (makes them louder). In Part 2, when you used the large bowl, you helped your Spy Ear pick up even more sound.

That's because the curved bowl takes all the sound waves that are coming toward it and reflects them at one point, called the focus. Bringing the waves together at one point makes them much louder, and if you put the Spy Ear right at that point, you'll hear a lot more. Microphones that use reflectors like this are called *parabolic microphones*.

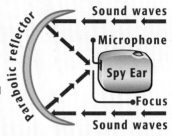

Parabolic microphones are used not only by secret agents, but also by film crews and bird-watchers (to hear bird songs). The parabolic microphones used by spies are much smaller than the one you created. With high-tech microphones, the reflector doesn't need to be any larger than a cereal bowl!

SPYquest

(continued from page 31)

You approach Mrs. Tulley after school and ask her if she has ever had a problem with Brad Barker.

"Brad *who?*" she asks.

"He lives down the street," you say. "You know, the *Barkers?*"

"Oh," she says. "*That* boy. The one who throws rocks at squirrels."

"Yes," you say, thinking you're on to something.

"He really has to stop that," she says, shaking her head. "Those poor squirrels."

"Have you ever had an argument with him?" you ask.

"Oh, no," she says. "I've rarely ever spoken to him. Why do you ask?"

■ Oh, well. It doesn't sound like this line of questioning is going anywhere. You'd better turn back and try something else!

OPERATION *Listen* UNDER!

In **Operation Talking Walls**, you learned that sound waves can travel though walls, but did you know they can also squeeze through little tubes? They sure *can*, and this operation will show you how your Spy Ear can team up with a drinking straw to *sip up* sounds from the space under a door. Does that sound cool? Read on to *hear* more!

STUFF YOU'LL NEED

- **Radio**
- 👓 **Spy Ear listening device**
- **Plastic drinking straw**

YOUR NETWORK

- **Two friends you can listen to**

WHAT YOU DO

1 Turn the radio on and set the volume at a medium level so that it's easily heard in the room.

2 Go outside the room and close the door. Notice how loud the radio is.

3 Place the Spy Ear's earphones in your ears, plug them into the earphone jack, switch on the Spy Ear, and turn the volume to a medium setting.

4 Point the microphone at the door. How loud is the radio now?

5 Slide the plastic straw between the bottom of the door and the floor so that one end of the straw enters the room.

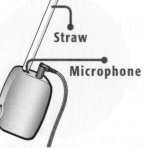

Straw

Microphone

6 Place the Spy Ear's microphone against the end of the straw. Make sure that the device is set at a medium volume and no louder (or it may squeak!). How well can you hear the radio now?

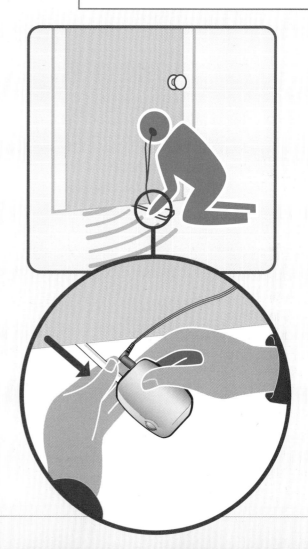

MORE FROM HEADQUARTERS

Try having your friends talk inside the room while you're behind a closed door. Can you hear what they're saying with your Spy Ear and the straw?

WHAT'S THE SECRET?

When you stick a straw under the door, the sound is transmitted through the straw and into the Spy Ear's microphone where it's amplified (or made louder). Real spies use this technique, but rather than simply go under doors, they can also listen through tiny holes in walls!

Working from the room next door, the spy drills a small hole through the wall in a spot where it won't be noticed easily. He then passes a hollow plastic tube through the hole until it reaches the other room. A sensitive microphone at the spy's end picks up and amplifies the sounds of voices in the room. The conversations are often recorded so they can be analyzed later.

PLASTIC TUBE

POWER CORD

MICROPHONE (INTERNAL)

This microphone can be used to listen through small holes in walls.

SPYquest

(continued from page 20)

You and your spy network keep up your surveillance of Mrs. Tulley's yard for a couple of hours, taking turns, but nothing else happens before you're all called home to dinner.

In the evening, you and Jeff are doing math homework together in your room, all the while keeping an eye on Mrs. Tulley's yard through the window. Everything's pretty quiet until Jeff says suddenly, "Did you hear that?"

"Hear what?"

"Shhhh," Jeff says and motions you toward the window. Both of you crouch beside it and look outside. Below, you can see a small orange animal digging around and tearing up plants in Mrs. Tulley's garden.

"What's that?" Jeff whispers.

And then the animal comes into full view.

"That's Mrs. Tulley's *cat!*" you whisper.

You've never seen the cat outside before, but sure enough, there she is!

■ If you decide to take a picture of the cat and confront Mrs. Tulley with the evidence, turn to **page 44.**

■ If you decide to tell Mrs. Tulley right now, turn to **page 41.**

OPERATION STOP Bugging ME

Do you want to bug your friends? Probably not—but this is a different kind of *bug*, and not the crawling kind, either. The **bugs** we're talking about are miniature listening devices that pick up the sound in a room and send it to a receiver at a **listening post** somewhere else. The bugs have to be hidden carefully in the room, though, or they'll be discovered, and that means trouble. See if you have what it takes to *bug* people by giving this operation a try!

STUFF YOU'LL NEED

- **Five plastic bottle caps**
- **Five 2-inch (5-cm) squares of aluminum foil**
- **Five 4-inch (10-cm) pieces of masking tape**
- **Watch or clock**

YOUR NETWORK

- **A friend to try to hunt for bugs in your room**

WHAT YOU DO

1 Place each bottle cap in the middle of a piece of foil. Fold the edges of the foil up to cover the bottle cap.

2 Make a loop in one piece of tape so that the sticky side is out. Stick the loop to the top of one bottle cap. Repeat for the other caps.

3 Have your friend leave the room for three minutes. While he's out of the room, hide the five bugs in various places around the room.

4 When your friend returns, give him ten minutes to find the bugs. If all the bugs aren't found in ten minutes, show him where they are.

5 Where were the bugs that were never found? Those are your best hiding places, so make a note of them. Why do you think those spots weren't checked?

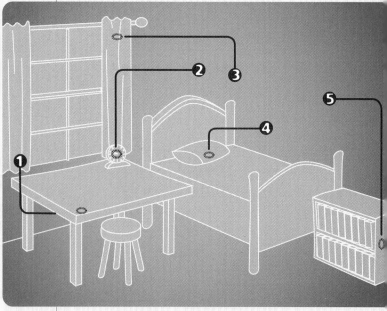

This tiny bug (shown larger than actual size) is only a little longer than a fingernail! It can be hidden behind a wall board, stashed above a ceiling panel, dangled down an air vent, or tucked into a lamp shade (or any other piece of furniture). It can go pretty much anywhere!

AIRWAY FOR MICROPHONE

MORE FROM HEADQUARTERS

Now switch roles with your friend! Have your friend hide the bugs while you're out of the room, and see if you can find them!

WHAT'S THE SECRET?

In real life, there are no rules about where you can hide a bug. The key is to put them in places where people talk and to hide them well enough that they won't be discovered. With advancements in technology, bugs are getting smaller and smaller, making them easier to hide and more difficult to find.

Here's a quick explanation of how a bug works. It has two main parts: a tiny *microphone* that picks up the sounds of people talking, and a *transmitter* that sends the sounds from the bug to a receiver at a listening post, usually in the form

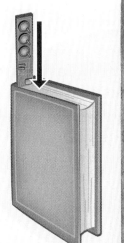

This microphone and transmitter can be slid into a book spine. That way, a bug can be hidden on a bookshelf!

of radio waves. The receiver takes the radio waves and turns them back into voices the same way a radio does.

A good bug should have a transmitter that sends a signal that's strong enough to be received at the spy's listening post, but weak enough so that it can't be easily located by anti-bugging devices, which scan for radio transmissions. Some of the latest computerized listening devices record conversations, store them for a short time, then transmit them to the listening post at a prearranged time. This reduces their chances of being detected, since they're not transmitting *all* the time.

AIRWAY FOR MICROPHONE

There is a bug hidden inside the plug of this extension cord! The airway for the microphone is so tiny it can hardly be seen.

(continued from page 17)

You spend the next hour walking the neighborhood. You see a lot of dogs, but they're all chained up or inside fenced yards. There are no dogs running free—at least *now* there aren't, anyway. You decide there's no point in continuing your search any longer.

■ This was a dead end. Go back and choose another route!

#13

Sound Wave

New high-tech listening devices let spies listen to the conversations in a room *without* using a **bug** or any kind of microphone at all. Instead, they use the power of light! It's high-tech and really cool. This operation will give you an idea of how it's done (with a little help from an empty yogurt cup, believe it or not!).

STUFF YOU'LL NEED

- **Small plastic yogurt cup (about 4 oz [113 g]) or any plastic cup of a similar size**
- **Scissors**
- **6 x 6-inch (15 x15-cm) piece of plastic wrap**
- **Rubber band**
- **Tape**
- **Flashlight**

YOUR NETWORK

- **A senior spy (an adult) to cut the cup**

WHAT YOU DO

1 Have the senior spy help you cut out the bottom of the yogurt cup with the scissors.

2 Next, place the plastic wrap over the mouth of the cup.

3 Stretch the plastic wrap tightly across the mouth of the cup, then hold it in place by placing the rubber band around the cup. Tape the edges of the wrap to the cup to ensure that the plastic wrap stays tight across the mouth of the cup.

4 Turn out the lights in the room and stand facing a wall. Use one hand to hold the cup, with the open end in front of your mouth.

5 Hold the flashlight (turned on) with your other hand. Aim the light toward the plastic wrap on the bottom of the cup so that the light reflects off of the plastic and onto the wall in front of you. Look at the shape of the reflected light on the wall.

6 Next, talk into the cup. Now what happens to the reflected light on the wall?

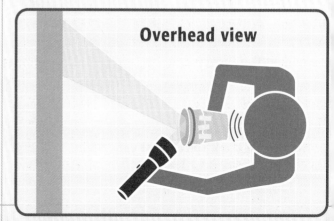

Overhead view

MORE FROM HEADQUARTERS

Say the same word several times into the cup and watch what happens to the reflected light. What do you notice? Try a different word. What do you notice now?

WHAT'S THE SECRET?

The reflected light on the wall will vibrate (move back and forth very rapidly) when you talk into the yogurt cup. That's because the sounds you make cause the air inside the cup to vibrate, which makes the plastic wrap vibrate as well. You can see those vibrations in the light reflected off the plastic wrap.

Just like the plastic wrap vibrates, *windows* vibrate when people talk in a closed room. New high-tech listening devices use laser light beams to detect this vibration. First, a laser beam is aimed at a window. The light bounces off the window and returns to a detector receiver and a computer. As the window vibrates, the laser's reflected light moves, and the computer converts those movements into the sounds that created them. And guess what—the windows still vibrate even when the blinds are closed or the shades are down! Bet you never thought your windows were so talkative!

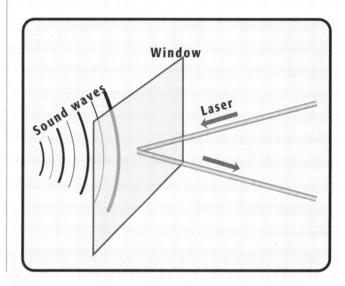

(continued from page 37)

You and Jeff run downstairs and head over to Mrs. Tulley's yard. When you get there though, the cat is nowhere to be found. She must have heard you coming and dashed away! You knock on the door and find that no one's home. How annoying!

The next morning, you march right over to Mrs. Tulley's house and knock on the door.

"I saw your cat digging up your garden last night!" you say when Mrs. Tulley answers the door.

"What are you talking about?" she says. "That's ridiculous!"

"But I saw it with my own eyes!" you say.

"Marigold doesn't go outside," Mrs. Tulley says. "She's a *housecat*! I'll bet it was your dog again!"

"I'm telling you, Ringo didn't do it!" you say.

"I saw him off his chain again yesterday!" Mrs. Tulley says. "Even *after* I made a special request to your mother that you keep him out of my yard!"

"Sorry," you say, because it is true that Ringo was off his chain last night.

But you *know* it was Marigold—if only you had some kind of proof!

"Can you at least check to see if Marigold has any dirt on her?" you ask.

"I assure you that Marigold is *spotless*," she says, picking up Marigold from her perch by the window. "She's the cleanest and most *dignified* cat you could ever imagine."

Indeed, you can see for yourself, Marigold's fur is soft and clean, with no trace of dirt.

■ This choice sure didn't get you anywhere! Go back and choose another path!

OPERATION

#14

give me a SIGN

I n **Operation Follow the Rabbit**, you learned how to use hand signals to communicate with your **tailing** team. But why stop there? Your hands can say a whole lot more! This operation will teach you how to use finger spelling (a form of sign language) to send any message you want. Try it, and see if this type of **code** comes in *handy*!

STUFF YOU'LL NEED
- **Just you and your hands**

YOUR NETWORK
- **A friend to receive your message**

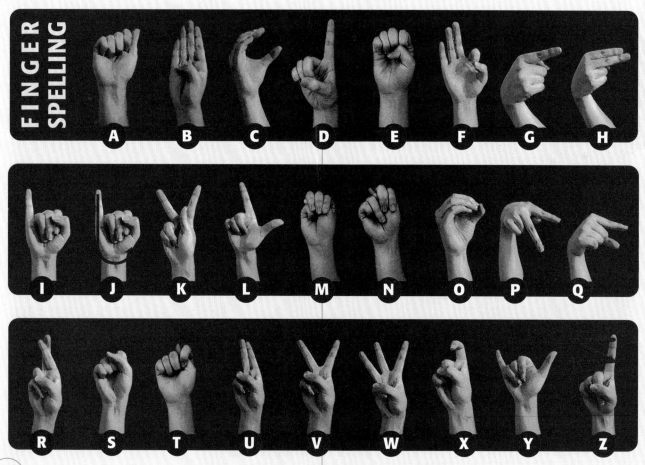

FINGER SPELLING

A B C D E F G H

I J K L M N O P Q

R S T U V W X Y Z

WHAT YOU DO

1 Study the chart of finger-spelling signs on page 42. Each sign stands for a different letter. Give them each a try to introduce your fingers to their new job. The letters are shown as the receiver of your message will see them. Practice with your hand facing you, and when it comes time to send a message, turn your hand to face your receiver.

2 Now's the tough part: Practice, practice, and practice some more, until you can remember the signs easily. Make sure your friend (who's going to be receiving your messages) does the same. This step will take a while, so be patient!

3 When you're ready to send your first message, have a friend sit across from you at a table.

4 Begin with both hands on the table. This means you're ready to start signing.

5 Now send your friend a secret message with your fingers! Say anything you want, but it'll be easiest if you start with a one-word message. If your message has more than one word, show the end of a word by holding the sign for the last letter a little longer than usual. If you have two of the same letter in a row, you can either sign the letter twice, or hold the sign and move your hand to the side in a bouncing motion.

SIGNING THE LETTER A

6 Your friend should translate the signs back into letters and then into words.

7 When you're done signing your message, ask your friend if it got across okay. How'd you do?

MORE FROM HEADQUARTERS

Can you translate this message? You can check your answer on page 48.

WHAT'S THE SECRET?

While finger spelling can be used by spies to send messages, it's not a *secret* code in the usual sense, since it's really a language for the deaf that quite a few people know. However, it's always good to have a way of sending a silent message across a room (or while you're outside on a tailing mission). The message is only at risk if you happen to be around a sign-language expert who has a direct view of your hands!

For extra security, you can develop your own codes using the letters. For example, the letter S could stand for "spy." Use your imagination and let your fingers do the talking!

SIGNING OFF!

Now that you know how to sign letters, expand your sign language skills by learning a few common words! That way, you can get your messages out a lot quicker. Here are some that might be useful for spy teamwork:

MEET · SECRET · DANGER

SPYquest

(continued from page 37)

You grab your camera and run outside. Hiding behind the corner of your house, you stick your arm out and snap several pictures of Mrs. Tulley's cat digging in the garden. Since you used your instinctive photography skills, the cat didn't get startled and run away.

First thing in the morning, you and Jeff have the film developed, and an hour later you have your photos. You have clear pictures of the cat with her paws deep in the dirt!

You head straight over to Mrs. Tulley's house and find her in the garden with her husband. You pull out the pictures and hand them to her.

"Ringo didn't dig up your flowers," you say. "It was your cat!"

Mrs. Tulley looks at the photos. She's at a loss for words at first, but then she says, "I'm very sorry I blamed Ringo, but I never imagined Marigold would go outside, much less dig up my garden!"

"I bet she's getting out through that hole in the porch screen," Mr. Tulley volunteers.

"I told you to get that fixed!" Mrs. Tulley snaps.

And so you leave Mr. and Mrs. Tulley to their squabbling. You've solved the mystery of the digger, and Ringo's out of trouble!

■ Congratulations! Quest accomplished!

Yes!

THE Thing AND THE TUNNEL

W orld War II (1939-1945) had barely ended before a whole new war—the Cold War—began. The two battling sides in the Cold War were democratic countries, led by the United States, and communist countries, led by the Soviet Union. This war was very different from other wars because most of the battles weren't "hot" battles fought with guns, but "cold" battles in which gaining access to information was the goal. Both sides used **espionage** as a main weapon.

One of the strangest and most original spy tools that the Soviet Union developed during this time was an audio device known simply as "The Thing."

On July 4, 1945, Soviet "Young Pioneers" (like the American Boy Scouts) presented a two-foot wooden carving of the Great Seal of the United States to American Ambassador Averell Harriman. The Great Seal featured a bald eagle holding an olive branch and thirteen arrows. But the gift was more than that. Beneath

A carved wooden copy of the Great Seal of the United States. A listening device was planted inside it by the Soviets!

THE THING

The back of the Great Seal with The Thing shown inside.

DIAPHRAGM

Sound waves

TUNING POST

ANTENNA

High-frequency radio beam

Reflected beam

Radio beams transmitted from a building nearby bounced off the diaphragm's antenna and were picked up by a receiver in the listening post. If people were talking in the room, the diaphragm would vibrate, creating electricity that would make the radio waves longer or shorter. These radio wavelengths could then be translated into what people in the office were saying.

the beak of the eagle, the Soviets had drilled one small hole that led to a sensitive listening device. The Soviets hoped that the seal would be proudly displayed in the ambassador's office, and sure enough, Mr. Harriman did just that. He hung the seal in his office in Spaso House, the ambassador's residence in Moscow. For seven years, the Soviets used the device to listen in on important discussions that the ambassador had in his office.

Then, in 1952, a routine security check revealed that the Great Seal held a bugging device that was activated by radio signals. At first, western experts had no idea how "The Thing" (the nickname given to the device) worked, because it had no batteries or electric circuits. It took a year and a half for a team of scientists to figure it out. Finally, British electronics specialist Peter Wright was able to make a copy of The Thing.

The Thing worked in an unusual way. The small hole below the eagle's beak led to a small space with a flexible front wall. The front wall (which was called a *diaphragm*) would vibrate when sound waves hit it, creating electric signals.

The United States didn't let on that it knew about The Thing until May 1960, when Ambassador Henry Cabot Lodge revealed the Great Seal bug at the United Nations. At that same time, he also said that more than a hundred similar devices had been recovered in American diplomatic buildings and residences in the Soviet Union and Eastern Europe.

THE BERLIN TUNNEL

While the Soviets were placing Things all over Europe, the United States was doing a little audio **surveillance** of its own in Germany. During the Cold War, Germany was divided into two parts: East Germany (which sided with the Soviets) and West Germany (which sided with the U.S. and its allies). The city of Berlin was also divided into east and west sides by a big wall called the Berlin Wall.

From 1954 to 1955, the CIA built a tunnel from West Berlin to East Berlin with help from the British foreign intelligence service, MI6. The Berlin Tunnel linked a building in West Berlin disguised as an American Air Force radar tower to underground communication cables used by the Soviet military in East Berlin. The tunnel was 1,476 feet (450 m) long, 6 feet (a little less than 2 m) high, and 15 feet (about 5 m) below the surface. For about a year, the United States bugged telephone conversations and discovered Soviet military strategies and other useful information. Then, on the morning of April 22, 1956, a team of technical specialists from the KGB (the Soviet intelligence service) broke into the East German end of the tunnel and the project ended.

Actually, the Soviets knew about the tunnel before it was even built, because British **mole** George Blake tipped them off in 1953. Soviet intelligence still decided to let the tunnel be built for two reasons. First of all, they wanted to protect Blake so that they could continue to get information from him. Second, they thought (incorrectly) that if they just tightened their security procedures, the CIA and MI6 wouldn't get any useful information.

The Cold War officially ended in 1991, when the Soviet Union dissolved into several smaller countries. But forty-five years of "cold" fighting led to huge advances in spy technology, and countries around the world are still developing more techniques to tap into each other's secrets. Who knows what the next big Thing will be!

The layout of the Berlin Tunnel built by the United States and Great Britain from 1954 to 1955. The tunnel was used to conduct audio surveillance on the Soviet military.

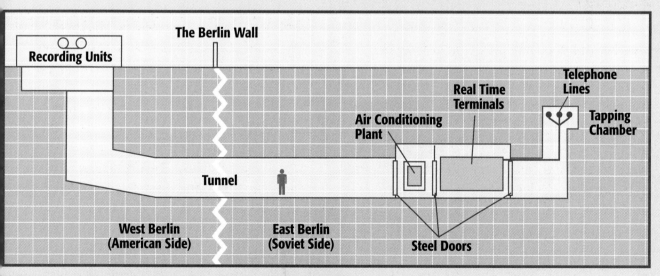

catch you later!

So, how's your spy vision? Sharper than 20/20? What about your ears—are they totally tuned in?

That's what we like to hear!

You've been completely immersed in the **tradecraft** of **surveillance** this month, and you've got a lot of new skills to show for it. You know how to build a **periscope** and a wide-angle viewer, and you also know how to amplify sound with special microphones (like the one in your trusty Spy Ear!). And let's not forget all the photography skills you *developed* with your new mini-camera!

You also learned a new set of hand signals and a special finger-spelling **code** that you can use to send secret messages when you're out on surveillance missions. As you've probably already guessed, those finger-spelling skills will help you figure out the end of the famous quote below. It's by Major George Beckwith, who was the head of British intelligence operations in the American colonies at the end of the American Revolutionary War (1775–1783). When he returned to England, after the British lost to General George Washington's army, Beckwith said:

"WASHINGTON DID NOT REALLY OUTFIGHT THE BRITISH, HE SIMPLY...

!"

Once you've figured out the end of the message (turn back to **Operation Give Me a Sign** on page 42 for help), you can check your answer in the Answer Spot on the right.

(turn back to **Operation Give Me a Sign** on page 42 for help)

We'll see you next month!

the answer spo